POPULAR PIANO SOLOS

Pop Hits, Broadway, Movies and More!

T0210300

PLAYBACK+
Speed • Pitch • Balance • Loop

The exclusive *Playback+* feature allows tempo changes without altering the pitch.
Loop points can also be set for repetition of tricky measures.

To access audio, visit:
www.halleonard.com/mylibrary

Enter Code
1590-2281-5906-1752

ISBN 978-1-4234-1255-7

WILLIS MUSIC

EXCLUSIVELY DISTRIBUTED BY

7777 W. BLUEMOUND RD. P.O. BOX 13819 MILWAUKEE, WI 53213

© 2006 by The Willis Music Co.
International Copyright Secured   All Rights Reserved

For all works contained herein:
Unauthorized copying, arranging, adapting, recording, Internet posting, public performance,
or other distribution of the printed or recorded music in this publication is an infringement of copyright.
Infringers are liable under the law.

Visit Hal Leonard Online at
www.halleonard.com

Contents

Till There Was You
from Meredith Willson's THE MUSIC MAN

Use with John Thompson's Modern Course for the Piano
FOURTH GRADE BOOK, after p. 15.

By Meredith Willson
Arranged by Glenda Austin

© 1950, 1957 (Renewed) FRANK MUSIC CORP. and MEREDITH WILLSON MUSIC
This arrangement © 2006 FRANK MUSIC CORP. and MEREDITH WILLSON MUSIC
All Rights Reserved

Moon River

from the Paramount Picture BREAKFAST AT TIFFANY'S

Use after page 19.

Words by Johnny Mercer
Music by Henry Mancini
Arranged by Glenda Austin

Copyright © 1961 (Renewed 1989) by Famous Music LLC
This arrangement Copyright © 2006 by Famous Music LLC
International Copyright Secured   All Rights Reserved

Imagine

Use after page 27.

Words and Music by John Lennon
Arranged by Glenda Austin

Gently and smoothly

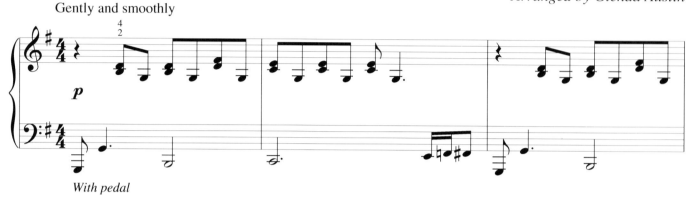

With pedal

© 1971 (Renewed 1999) LENONO.MUSIC
This arrangement © 2006 LENONO.MUSIC
All Rights Controlled and Administered by EMI BLACKWOOD MUSIC INC.
All Rights Reserved   International Copyright Secured   Used by Permission

Somewhere Out There

from AN AMERICAN TAIL

Use after page 35.

Music by Barry Mann and James Horner
Lyric by Cynthia Weil
Arranged by Glenda Austin

Copyright © 1986 USI A MUSIC PUBLISHING and USI B MUSIC PUBLISHING
This arrangement Copyright © 2006 USI A MUSIC PUBLISHING and USI B MUSIC PUBLISHING
All Rights Controlled and Administered by UNIVERSAL MUSIC CORP. and SONGS OF UNIVERSAL, INC.
All Rights Reserved   Used by Permission

12

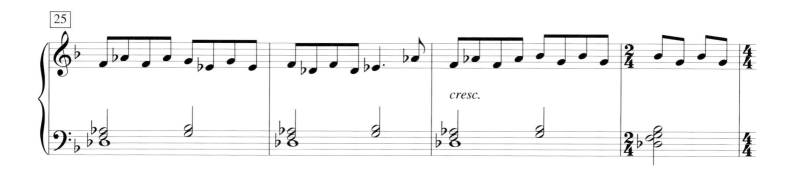

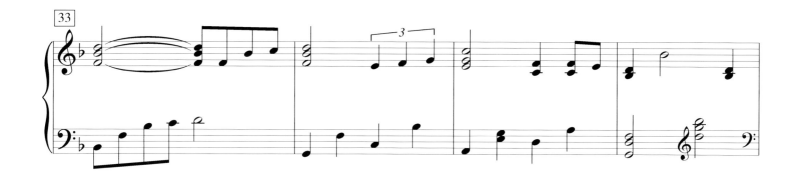

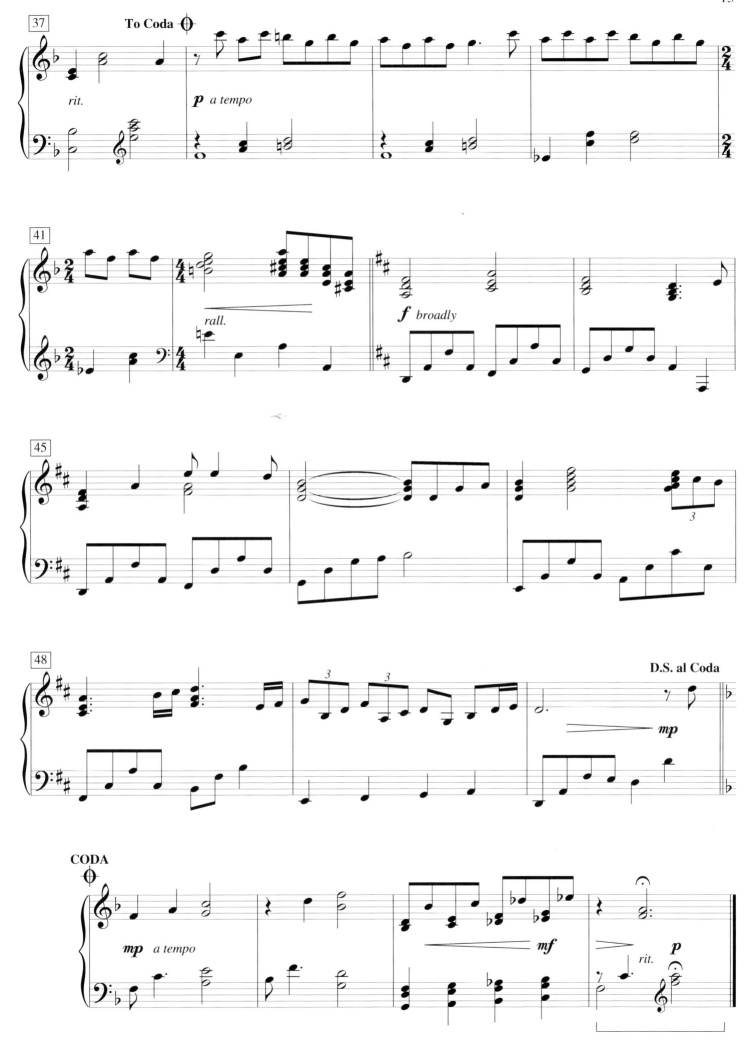

On Broadway

Use after page 43.

Words and Music by Barry Mann,
Cynthia Weil, Mike Stoller and Jerry Leiber
Arranged by Glenda Austin

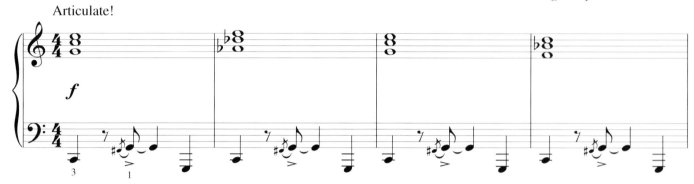

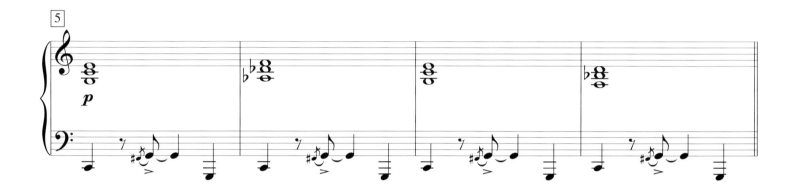

© 1962, 1963 (Renewed 1990, 1991) SCREEN GEMS-EMI MUSIC INC.
This arrangement © 2006 SCREEN GEMS-EMI MUSIC INC.
All Rights Reserved   International Copyright Secured   Used by Permission

Chariots of Fire

Use after page 57.

Music by Vangelis
Arranged by Glenda Austin

© 1981 EMI MUSIC PUBLISHING LTD.
This arrangement © 2006 EMI MUSIC PUBLISHING LTD.
All Rights for the World, excluding Holland, Controlled and Administered by EMI APRIL MUSIC INC.
All Rights Reserved   International Copyright Secured   Used by Permission

Endless Love

Use after page 71.

Words and Music by Lionel Richie
Arranged by Glenda Austin

With much expression

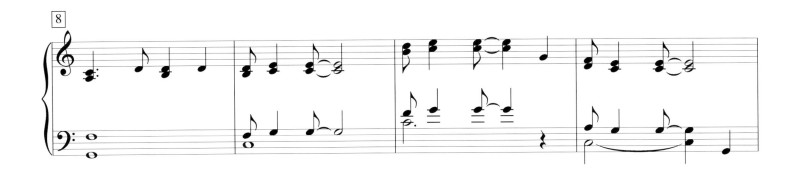

Copyright © 1981 by PGP Music, Brockman Music and Brenda Richie Publishing
This arrangement Copyright © 2006 by PGP Music, Brockman Music and Brenda Richie Publishing
All Rights for PGP Music Administered by Intersong U.S.A., Inc.
International Copyright Secured   All Rights Reserved

A Whole New World
from Walt Disney's ALADDIN

Use after page 83.

Music by Alan Menken
Lyrics by Tim Rice
Arranged by Glenda Austin

Not too fast, gently rhythmic

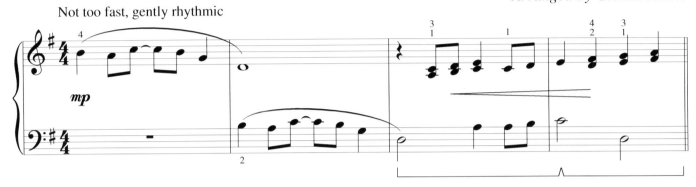

With pedal

© 1992 Wonderland Music Company, Inc. and Walt Disney Music Company
This arrangement © 2006 Wonderland Music Company, Inc. and Walt Disney Music Company
All Rights Reserved   Used by Permission

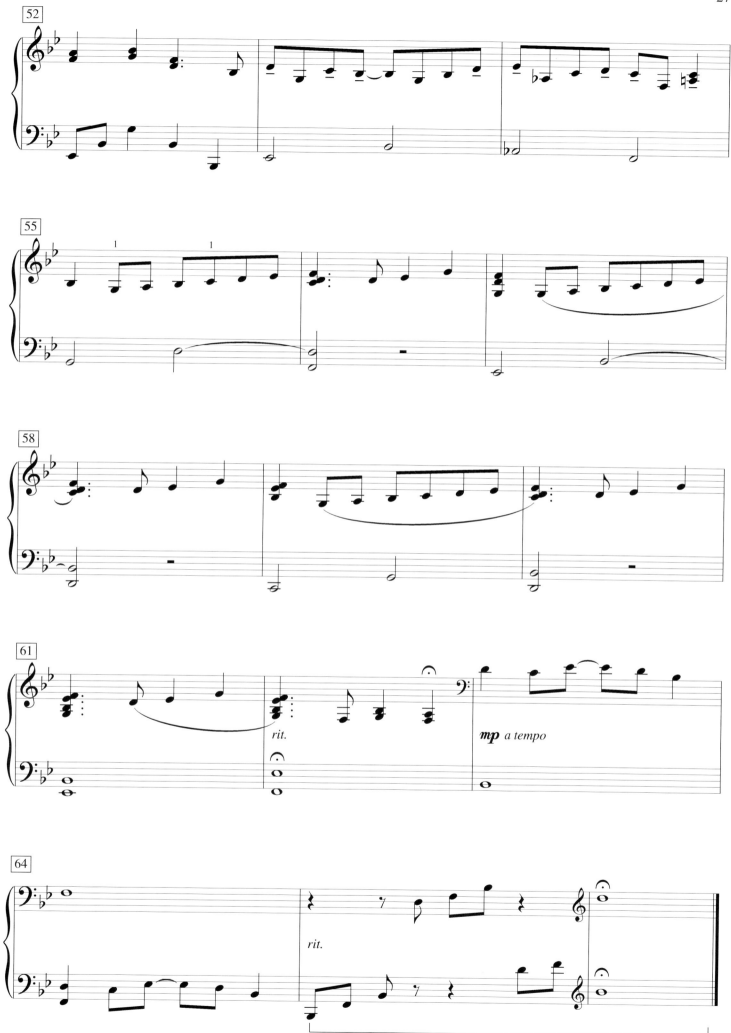

Mission: Impossible Theme

from the Paramount Television Series MISSION: IMPOSSIBLE

Use after page 92.

By Lalo Schifrin
Arranged by Glenda Austin

Accented, with drive

Copyright © 1966, 1967 (Renewed 1994, 1995) by Bruin Music Company
This arrangement Copyright © 2006 by Bruin Music Company
International Copyright Secured   All Rights Reserved

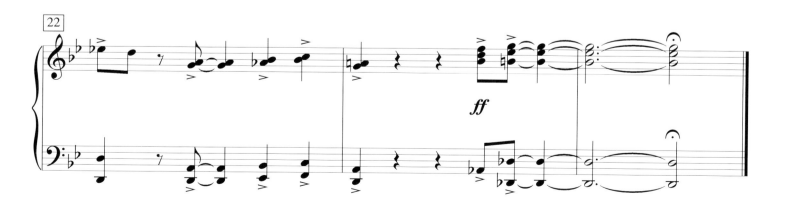

Seasons of Love

from RENT

Use after page 92.

Words and Music by Jonathan Larson
Arranged by Glenda Austin

© 1996 FINSTER & LUCY MUSIC LTD. CO.
This arrangement © 2006 FINSTER & LUCY MUSIC LTD. CO.
All Rights Controlled and Administered by EMI APRIL MUSIC INC.
All Rights Reserved   International Copyright Secured   Used by Permission